Lost Innocence

My Journey from Addiction to Recovery

Merrit Hartblay

Published by Merrit Hartblay

4 2nd Street

Greenvale, NY 11548

Manufactured in the United States of America

ISBN 9798670647342 paperback

ACKNOWLEDGEMENTS

This book is dedicated to all of the people who have struggled with drug addiction, the strong ones who keep coming back to 12 step meetings and to the families who never give up, as well as the countless men and women who have dedicated their lives to understanding and treating addiction at rehabs, hospitals and outpatient treatment centers. To the people who have traveled in my footsteps who, when they have fallen, have been able to let themselves rise from the ashes to rebuild their lives. One of the greatest gifts of sobriety is having the chance to live two lives in one lifetime!

This book is dedicated to my loving and caring family, especially my son Trevor, who has been a huge part of my sobriety. To my dear friends Al Voss, Gary Truce and Betty Ann Gaube and the rest of my Binghamton University family. To my dear friend Peter Hoppenfeld, who was there for me at the lowest point of my life and lifted me up so that I could find the path to recovery. To my dear sister Sharon, who has been there for me during my darkest times.

To Claudia Ragni, who has always supported me and been there for me as well as the entire Ken Peters Center for Recovery family. To Louise Hay, whose teachings encouraged me to never give up, to challenge myself to be the person I was always meant to be. To my entire AA family without whose support, this book would not have been published. To Mark Armiento, who taught me that you need to always follow your heart and to never let anyone tell you what you can or cannot do - to always know where Waldo is! To my family at Outreach who gave me the best drug counseling education possible and later the opportunity to give it back by becoming a lecturer and student advisor.

And finally, to Jess. Our paths crossed as a godsend. This book would not have been published if not for her wisdom and guidance and her belief in me! I am very grateful!

To the countless individuals out there who never stopped believing in me, my gratitude goes to you.

We are all on this journey together!

CHAPTER 1
THE BEGINNING

Reflecting on how I had gotten to this place in my life. This was one of the hardest things I ever had to do, but it was the first step that I had to take to begin to free myself from my past.

September 24th, 2008, 2:00am.

I have been sleeping on the couch in the living room for over a year now. My son is up in his room and his mother is in hers. Unable to sleep, I am drinking from a bottle of vintage port wine; trying to understand how and why my life had unraveled. I had been out of work now for several months and drinking had become my new hobby.

My most recent job was again, "a dream job"; but like those before, I had sabotaged it because my ego and self-will got in the way. It has pretty much been like this ever since June 22, 2002, when the company I was working for, WorldCom, took a mighty tumble and literally went from Chapter 7 to Chapter 11 overnight.

I had been a senior level manager at the time and had accumulated a significant amount of stock options over the years. At WorldCom, management success was recognized by rewarding stock options. Foolishly, I had put all my savings and bonus monies back into the company and the 401K plan. When the end came, I lost everything. I went from a six-figure salary to unemployment and I fell with a mighty thud.

Up to this point, I didn't think my drinking was a problem, but it had now become one. I drank in order to become comfortably numb. My wife had a hard time understanding why this had happened and pretty much blamed everything on me. As I have come to learn, being emotionally abused is so much worse than physical abuse - you can fix a broken arm, but a broken soul is something else entirely.

My father had always taught me that when life kicks you in the butt, you picked yourself up, brushed off the dirt and start again. And so, I did, several times.

The telecommunications Industry was going through tough times and venture capital was being thrown around like confetti; investors hoping to catch the next big wave. I went from company to company trying to reinvent myself, but it just wasn't working. In the past, I was always able to "juggle" all the balls: taking care of the family; paying the bills, etc., but now all the balls were falling. My self-esteem was at an all-time low. The liquid courage that had been running through my veins for so long was no longer doing the job.

I had recently had shoulder surgery, and pain killers had now entered the picture. Vicodin and Tequila seemed to do the job and had become my new best friends.

We lived a few blocks from the bay, which was off the Long Island Sound, so my daily sojourn down to the beach included a backpack filled with a batch of screwdrivers, a few joints, and a bottle of pills. Self-pity combined with being out of work had taken me to a very dark place. I just couldn't seem to grab on to any sane thoughts. I had a loving son who I cherished, and I couldn't even be there for him.

Every once in a while, I would put on a suit and give the impression that I was heading off to the city for a job interview, but all I did was head to my favorite watering holes and spend the afternoon and most nights drinking and playing darts. I had been frequenting one particular bar for almost twenty years, and it had become my second home. I was safe there and no one judged me.

Most days, I got home after dinner and just isolated. I didn't want to be seen or talk to anyone. I even pushed my own son away from me, and I am quite sure that at this point he had had it with me. I had always tried to be there for him.

I coached little league Baseball for almost ten years.

I remember teaching my son how to throw a baseball and ride a bicycle.

My son was everything to me.

When WorldCom collapsed in 2002, so did my marriage. I had done my best to be a good husband, but now, I was in no position to provide for my family and my wife took on the role of sole provider.

I was starting to have daily thoughts of suicide and was making late night calls to my sister and mother, trying to say goodbye. I knew deep down inside that I couldn't hurt myself, but the thoughts were enough to scare me and my family. I remember many nights, sitting in my jeep at the town dock, thinking about driving off into the water. The only sane thought that stopped me was that I didn't want to leave my son without a father.

The days just seemed to slip by, drifting into weeks, then months, then years. I had become a hermit in my own house. I tried to pull myself up and find the strength to move forward, but the pity party I was living in was too overwhelming.

September 24th, 2008.

The day started out like most of my days back then; a few quick drinks to greet the day, then driving my son up to the high school. By 7:30am, I was back at home, still unemployed, sitting in front of the television set, watching "Little House on the Prairie", drinking a few more eye openers, crying and wondering how I had gotten here.

The "poor me's" had become my staple diet. I was fifty-four years old, married, with a son, and having those daily horrible thoughts; not wanting to live and not wanting to die.

How did this happen?

I was born in 1954 and grew up in Jamaica, New York. I lived with my parents in a one-bedroom apartment, my parents sleeping on the pull-out couch in the living room. My sister was born four years later. Our family unit was now complete. I have very vivid memories of my childhood. My mother was one of six and my father one of four, so I had a huge extended family. Weekends were spent shuffling between the Bronx and Brooklyn, visiting both sets of relatives.

My parents always argued a lot; nothing physical, but verbal abuse ran high, especially with my mother always putting down my father. It was at an early age that I first saw how alcohol seemed to be the medicine that both my parents needed to get them through their collective days.

My father would return from a hard day's work in the Garment Center and have a few drinks to relax, my mother always joining him. We always lived in an apartment, and with the four of us, it was always close quarters. My sister and I always shared a bedroom, separated only by desks and bookshelves. Those days were a challenge. Escaping to the school yards was my daily reprieve from the arguments that my parents had. I guess, looking back, it became the norm. My friends and I would play ball - basketball, baseball, football - until it was too dark to see, and then I would hop on my trusty three-speed Tour de France bicycle and ride home. Staying out of the house became by weekly goal.

When I was about nine years old, I remember hitting my sister with a metal loom. We were making potholders, and I was mad at her. She wouldn't leave me alone. Looking back, it saddens me to remember how I treated her. I should have loved her more back then. I was jealous of her.

I also remember once convincing my sister that she was adopted. We had always shared a room and I wanted my own room. I remember my sister crying and I didn't care; how selfish of me. How could a brother do that to his sister?

I loved my sister and I wasted so many years being jealous of her. My sister had more friends than I did, and I was lonely. My parents were seemingly in their own world, and all it did was make me angry.

My sister and I had to fend for ourselves, watching out for each other. When we were old enough, we babysat for each other while my parents were off with their friends, dining and drinking. I remember waiting up at night, looking out the bedroom window, looking to see if their car was coming down the street. We never knew what kind of mood my parents would be in when they walked through the door. Inevitably, it was clear that they had been drinking, the smell of alcohol permeating the apartment.

My mother would be fighting with my father about one thing or another. I felt bad for my dad; he just took whatever my mother dished out.

I remember one time that my mother tried cutting her wrists. Some people came and took her off to the hospital. It was something that I will never forget. My sister was too young at the time to remember; thank god for that.

Years later, I had the chance to talk to my mother about this, and all she could do was hang her head. My mother did finally admit to me and my sister that she wished that she had never had any children. We had turned out to be inconveniences.

My parents would take many trips away with their friends to Las Vegas and Aruba, and my sister and I spent most of our childhood spending weekends with our aunt and uncle and our two cousins at their house on Long Island. We both loved staying there; we felt safe, warm, and loved.

I remember coming home from my freshman year of college and taping all my record albums shut so that my sister couldn't use them. She was so mad at me. I didn't care; I didn't want anyone using my records. I hated my sister for having to share a room with her. I had no privacy. I should have been more compassionate and understanding.

As I look back now, it is clear to me that I had developed addictive behavior long before alcohol and drugs would eventually come into my life.

I remember the late night car rides home from Brooklyn on the weekends, my father speeding as he always did, navigating the tight turns on the then Interboro Parkway. My sister and I would huddle down on the floor of the backseat, praying that we would arrive home safe.

Those rides went on well into my teens, my mother yelling at my father, shouting at him to slow down and threatening to throw herself from the car. On one occasion, she actually opened her car door while the car was speeding along, and I remember my father reaching over and pulling her back into the car. No child should have memories like those.

I don't want to only paint a bleak picture. There were a lot of good times.

I grew up in a Queens's neighborhood where we had friends on every block. Tar beach (the rooftop of our apartment building) was our summer, all the moms sitting out on their folding chairs, while all the kids played, sometimes blocks away. Every kid knew their mom's yell. It was a simple time. The summer air smelled sweet and the snow falls were plenty in the winter.

I remember the taste of the snowflakes on my tongue. It should have been a time of innocence, but it wasn't. With thirteen first cousins, weekend family gatherings were frequent. In addition to my parents' drinking, my aunts and uncles and older cousins also drank. It seemed like the thing to do.

The fights and arguments were all too frequent. It was due to this that I remember at age thirteen/fourteen saying that I would never drink alcohol.

My older cousins and uncles had to physically carry my father out of the reception hall at the end of my Bar Mitzvah celebration. I swore that I would never drink and actually wrote it down on a piece of paper, signing it. Who would have thought?

During my early years, my parents would take me and my sister away for the summers to the Catskill Mountains (upstate New York), Monticello, to be exact - the "Jewish Alps". We stayed in Bungalow Colonies; my father driving up on Friday afternoon and returning to the city on Sunday night. Those were very special times.

I loved fishing with my father on the lake and playing softball on the weekend against the other local Bungalow Colonies. Funny, as I look back now, I do remember always finding it hard to fit in with the other kids; always feeling like I was on the outside looking in. I did everything I could to be accepted.

The times I dreaded the most were when Labor Day weekend approached, signaling the end of summer vacation. It was a long ride home. The summers seemed like an eternity and going back home was such a sad time.

I made it through high school and couldn't wait to go away to college. I hated the fact that I would be leaving my sister behind to fend for herself; but all I wanted to do was to get away. Sports had always been my passion and I was able to get a track scholarship to the State University of New York at Binghamton. You can imagine what campus life was like in the 1970's. Thankfully, I had an amazing coach who kept me focused.

Coach Truce changed my life, and we remain close friends to this day. Coach always emphasized that academics come first, and I stayed focused for almost three and a half years. I prided myself on getting my varsity jacket and actually had real pennies in my penny loafers. My teammates called me "Wally Cleaver".

I did find some other passion such as acting, and music, and I was able to become a disc jockey on the campus radio station. I also did play-by-play on radio for the school basketball team for home and away games.

My freshman year of college, I invited my girlfriend, who was at another university on Long Island, up to visit for a weekend. My intention was to break up with her.

I had recently met someone else, and as sick as this sounds, wanted to get my girlfriend's approval. I made up a story that the girl I had just met was actually going out with my roommate and asked her what she thought. As I have since learned many times over, the grass is not always greener on the other side. I was so selfish, and I treated my girlfriend so badly. It was all about me and my ego.

I loved her so much and all I did was hurt her. What was wrong with me? I feel so badly about how I behaved. I realize now that my bad behavior and lack of maturity may have been attributed to the fact that I was the child of alcoholics, not ever having been taught healthy coping skills.

Junior year, at an important track meet, I let my team down by faking an injury during a major race. I had fallen behind and couldn't accept losing. Again, my ego got in the way and my pride took over.

It was in my second year of recovery that I finally started to come to terms with being an ACOA (Adult Child of an Alcoholic). It is easier for me to look back at my childhood and adolescent years and recognize why I developed the defense mechanisms that would eventually carry me through my adult years.

Back in sixth grade, I remember using my bank book money to buy pizza for my friends. I told my father that I had gotten into a fight and that the money had been stolen. My father didn't believe me and, for the first time ever, he hit me and sent me flying across the floor. I finally told the truth. I was mad at my father for never giving me enough pocket money and for not doing things with me on the weekends.

My father was always too busy doing the daily crossword puzzle and sipping on a cocktail. I used to yell at him and beg him to go out and do something with me. He would make me cry. I wound up taking it out on my sister. I hurt her time and time again.

My teenage summers were spent working as a counselor at a Long Island day camp. I had great times back then. It was probably the summer of my junior year of college that I tried alcohol for the first time. At first, I didn't like it because it brought back too many bad memories. After a while, I liked the way it made me feel. It made me feel warm all over and also made it easier to fit in and talk to girls. All the while, my parents were still drinking and doing whatever they could to remain comfortably numb.

I graduated college in 1976, and it was time to go out and find a career. I had wanted to get into the broadcasting industry, so I put together a resume and started pounding the streets of New York City, filling out job applications at all the major broadcast networks and radio stations. It was at the CBS Broadcast Network that I landed my first job, in the corporate payroll department. My plan was to just get my foot inside the door.

One of my job responsibilities was to deliver weekly time sheets to all the departments: news, sports, records, and advertising. I started to make strong contacts and wound up having the opportunity to do free-lance work on the weekends for CBS Sports, working alongside some of my broadcasting idols.

Within one year, I was hired to work in Network Operations. This division was responsible for bringing all the news and sports feeds from around the globe back into New York for distribution to all the local television affiliates. I had some amazing mentors who taught me all they knew about television broadcasting.

It was a very special time for me. CBS was at the pinnacle. The news and record divisions were at the top of their respective fields.

Half the building, known as "Black Rock," smoked pot while the other half drank martinis. Lunch time progressed from pitchers of beer at Brew Burger to martinis at the 21 Club. Drinking during the day was acceptable, but it was during happy hour, when everyone cut loose.

For me, I would hurry home on the subway to play some hoops, and then it was a quick shower and a change of clothes and back to the city for play time and dancing at the disco's, three to four nights a week at Studio 54, Xenon, Le Mouche and New York, New York. It was during this time that I was introduced to cocaine; it helped me stay up longer so I could drink more.

Chapter Two

Career Emerging

Reflecting back on my early careers, I came to realize that I always wound up self-sabotaging good situations. Never really understanding that inside, I never believed that I deserved good things to happen in my life.

Everyone I knew worked hard but played harder. It was an innocent time. Cocaine did lead to other drugs. but never to excess. I know now that I, like my parents, was staying comfortably numb. I seemed to just be going through life; doing what was expected of me.

Summers had now shifted to the beach clubs of Long Island. I loved being by the water; it was the perfect place to hang out with friends. I might call some of those summers the summers of Quaaludes - everyone I know did them. It seemed like pills and alcohol were the perfect concoction. All my inhibitions seemed to slip away.

My parents shared a cabana at the beach club on the south shore of Long island with some of their close friends who, like them, loved their alcohol. They drank throughout the weekend days and well into the night.

My father played poker with his friends on the roof top deck most of those weekends, and when I was younger, I would sit next to him and watch them play. I remember my father once said to me that one day I would acquire a taste for scotch, as if was a rite of passage. The summers seemed to slide right by, everyone just finding their own way to "get by".

Looking back, it never really felt like anyone was really happy with their lives. They all put on the perfect disguises.

I remember when I got one of my first jobs. I came home and my father asked me how it went. I said okay, but that I wasn't really happy. My father replied, "what does work have to do with being happy?" I will never forget that. It seemed that most people I knew, including my parents, worked hard but were not happy. Funny, but now I couldn't imagine feeling any other way.

One summer, my sister got married and the pressure was really on. Everyone kept asking me "so when are you going to find a nice girl and settle down?" Some friends of my parents at the beach club had a daughter close to my age.

We started dating one summer, and before I knew it, I was looking out at three hundred guests at my wedding. I remember my best friend, my best man, coming up to me just as we were getting ready to walk down the aisle, handing me his car keys and telling me to run as fast as I could and not look back. Needless to say, my soon to be mother-in-law, almost had a fit. I should have listened to him.

After the ceremony, while everyone was dancing, eating and drinking, I was downstairs in one of the Hebrew School classrooms with some close friends doing lines of cocaine, getting as numb as possible. Is that anyway to enjoy your wedding day?

I was a middle-class kid from Queens. My new in-laws were wealthy Long Islander's living in a huge house, not far from the ocean. Suffice it to say, it was a dicey relationship.

My father-in-law's idea of a Sunday afternoon was smoking cigars, going out on the boat, and discussing Wall Street. All I wanted to do was watch football and get stoned.

It was a two-year roller-coaster ride. In the end, I couldn't live up to my wife's and in-laws' expectations. It took all the strength I could muster to walk away.

I remember the day vividly. It was a Saturday and summertime, and we were getting ready to head out to the beach. I was sitting at the dining room table rolling a batch of joints for the day. My wife was filling a vile of cocaine. I asked her to sit down; that I had something to tell her. I said that it was clear that we were both unhappy with the way our marriage was going and that something had to be done.

I told her that I needed to go downstairs for a few minutes and that she should think about what I had said. I went down to the bank and withdrew all the money in our account, three thousand dollars. I came back upstairs, sat down at the table and split up the money. I gave her half and said that this was the end and that it was time to go our separate ways. I never gave her a chance to speak her mind. I told her that I would take a few things and find a place to stay for a few days, while she sorted things out.

The following days and weeks were nothing short of a nightmare. When I finally returned a few days later to get some more of my things; the locks to the apartment had been changed. So, being full of resentments and anger, I had the electricity turned off. The ensuing divorce was equally nightmarish.

I found an attorney (Jacoby & Meyers) behind the men's clothing racks at Times Square Stores. My father-in-law brought in his five hundred dollar a day, Park Avenue attorney. You do the math. All I wanted was my golf clubs and record albums.

I was miserable and couldn't stand it anymore. I never once thought about working things out and going for marriage counseling. All I thought about was myself. It was a tough time for me. Thank God that we didn't have any children. Once again, alcohol and drugs seemed to make things better. I had not been the husband and son-in-law that everyone had hoped for.

It was around this time that I had the distinct feeling that I was being followed. My father-in-law was wealthy and well known in certain circles, and me hurting his daughter was not well received. On a few occasions, I found my car broken into, and I began feeling paranoid that someone was out to get me. I had refused to give my wife a Jewish divorce (Get) - which meant that we would have to go before a panel of rabbis - and that made things all the worse. I finally surrendered to all the pressure and gave everyone what they wanted. We had been living in Great Neck, New York at the time, and all I wanted to do was to get as far away as possible.

A friend of mine owned an apartment in Queens (as an investment) and worked things out so that I could move in. I had just landed a job in telecommunications with one of the major brokerage houses with offices at the World Trade Center. The night life of the city came calling.

My best friend and his girlfriend lived in the West Village and every night was a party. I was hanging out with photographers and models; my best friend's girlfriend was a booking agent for a well-known modeling agency, and I had nightly invites to the hottest parties in town.

After work it was over to the bars on First Avenue for drinks and late-night parties. Although the parties went on well into the wee hours, I always managed to find my way back apartment in Queens and show up for work the next day on time. Looking back, I can see now how "clouded" my vision was. I just seemed to be going through the motions, never stopping to truly appreciate the jobs that I had.

In the early 1980's, I was offered an Adjunct Professor's position at New York University. I had been asked to develop and teach a course in Broadcast Operations and Satellite Communications. I was thrilled. The course was a huge success, and I was subsequently offered to teach similar courses at Manhattan Marymount and St. John's University.

I was working hard during the day, teaching part-time and partying into the night. One of the harshest realizations in later years was knowing that I lived most of my life, based on other people's expectations for me, and when things didn't work out, the feeling of failure always set in. This always led to rounds of depression and a case of the "poor me's."

The telecom job I had suddenly and abruptly came to an end as the direction of the company was changing, and my position phased out. My first thoughts were that maybe this was the time to leave New York. Strangely enough, a few weeks later I received a call from an industry associate. My friend was building a huge telecommunications facility in Houston, Texas, and he asked me if I might be interested in coming to work for him. I had significant broadcast network contacts which would prove invaluable.

I was flown down to Houston and given the red-carpet treatment. I fell in love with the city almost instantly. I always loved horses and wanted to be just like "Bobby Ewing" from the hit show "Dallas". Terms were worked out, and I flew back to New York to close that chapter of my life.

It was close to New Year's and I wanted to say goodbye to my closest friends. I bought two cases of champagne (Vive Clicquot - my favorite) and delivered them personally. I was packed in two days. The moving truck came, and I flew out of La Guardia airport to start the next and hopefully better chapter of my life.

Chapter Three
Moving Away

I now had the feeling that, if I moved away and started anew, that everything in my life would be okay. Little did I know that, wherever you go, you take yourself with you!

Moving to Texas was like being in a dream; so far removed from New York; an entirely different way of life.

I gave up my wing tips for lizard skin cowboy boots and my baseball cap for a Stetson. The company put me up in a hotel until I could find a place to live. They also gave me a company car (part of the deal) so that I could get around town.

What a change. I was no longer disco dancing. I quickly learned the Texas Two-Step and the Cotton-Eyed Joe. The only thing that was the same was the crazy night life. I found my way around Houston pretty quickly and soon felt right at home.

On the work front, we had landed some huge contracts with some of the world's largest oil companies, building telecommunications infrastructures for them from their oil rigs out in the Gulf back to Houston. It was a very exciting time. Additionally, we had a fleet of mobile satellite trucks that were being booked out by the major broadcast networks for sports and news coverage.

The kid from Queens was now riding high in the saddle. Happy hour was a big event in Houston, and before too long, tequila became my new best friend.

As I have since learned in years of recovery, even if you move to another city, you always take yourself with you. I had made some close friends in a short time, and they loved to party; pot and cocaine were not far behind. I didn't have to wear suits anymore. Cowboy wranglers and button downs worked just fine. I was living the life in Texas and New York seemed like a lifetime ago.

Houston had a great night life; jazz clubs, dance halls and plenty of women. I was riding horses almost every day and partying it up every night. I had moved away, hoping to find serenity. Instead, all the craziness in my life followed me. No matter how late into the night I was out, true to form, I always showed up for work the next day, on time.

The projects with the oil companies were bringing in significant revenue and we started working with some major real estate developers. Telecommunications, as an industry, was at the forefront, and I was smack dab in the middle. I was traveling all across the country, meeting with the broadcast networks and lining up additional projects. Things could not have been any better.

Although the company was doing well, it became clear that there were some internal issues going on that were causing some friction. Once again, my work situation took a sudden and unexpected turn.

One of my associates, who I had known before coming to Houston, and who I had become close friends with, was abruptly fired. Ray had been responsible for a good amount of our network business and had recently signed a huge contract with ESPN for the use of our mobile satellite trucks for a series of sporting events.

Faced with the sudden loss of his job, Ray took a leap of faith and purchased a satellite truck on his own and started his own company. Hearing about this, the CEO of my company instructed me to contact ESPN and confirm that we still had the business they had committed to with Ray. When I reached my contact at ESPN, he informed me that he had already spoken to Ray and had agreed to give him a shot at the business that he had previously booked with our company. I understood completely, because in our industry, loyalty was everything (or so I thought).

I went back to my CEO and informed him of ESPN's decision. Needless to say, he was outraged and directed me to contact senior management at ESPN and have our contact fired for breaking his agreement. One thing I have always been, especially when it comes to business, is ethical, sincere, and loyal. I was not going to stab a dear friend in the back.

After thinking about it over a few shots of tequila, I wrote out my resignation letter and handed it in.

So, the company car was gone, and all I had to get around town with was my trusty, three speed bicycle. Can you picture that, peddling around Houston with lizard skin boots and a Stetson? That was something. After considering my options, I decided that I would stay around for a while and find some work. I had a new set of friends, so why leave?

I wound up getting a bartending job and also found some part-time security work at some of the clubs. I felt like a million dollars; drinking for free and hanging out all night with the Texas beauties. I had family back in New York, but never thought about going home.

As bartending goes, it didn't take long before cocaine came into play on a daily basis. Cocaine gave me the ability to stay up longer. As I mentioned earlier, happy hours were all the rage back then. Floor long buffets and free drinks from 4-6pm. I met up with all my buddies at 4pm every day.

I remember being at a club one night. It was close to midnight, and I had just gotten off work. I spotted a lady and asked her if I could buy her a drink. She said that she had to go somewhere to help a friend out but that I could come by her place at around 2am - how do you say no? She gave me her number and address and we agreed to meet later on.

I later went home to freshen up and made it to her apartment right on time. I knocked on the door, and when it opened, there stood a lady in a black teddy drinking Jack Daniels out of a bottle. I thought that I must have been in a car accident on the way over and had died and went to heaven. We embarked on a heated romance and things really started to get crazy.

My new lady friend was living with a cocaine dealer, and before too long, drugs seemed to override alcohol. Before I knew what happened, we were in front of the Justice-of-the-Peace getting married. We had been together for almost one month.

I remember going to the local department store to get wedding rings. They asked us when we needed them, and we said in one hour. It was a whirlwind romance.

Before we had met, my new wife had been seeing an old boyfriend from back home in Pittsburgh. When he found out we were dating, he tracked me down to the bar where I was working, and we almost came to blows.

My wife and I moved in together and things seemed to be going pretty well. I was still bartending and doing security work, and she was working full time for a real estate title company. The drinking and drugging reached a fever pitch.

I wasn't very happy with the work I was doing and started to think about going back to New York. My wife was in agreement, so I worked on updating my resume. I flew back to New York several times for job interviews, and within two months, I had been offered a consulting job with a high-tech research firm. My wife resigned from her job, and in a matter of days, we were packed up and headed back east.

The trip took us about three days. We stopped in Pittsburgh to visit her parents and her extended family. It was the first time I had met them, and I felt right at home.

They lived in a small town about 25 miles north of Pittsburgh and it was like being in "Mayberry". I took to my in-laws almost immediately, and we had a great visit. We spent about a day with them and then headed on to New York. We would be staying with my parents until we could find a place of our own.

Chapter 4

New York Stories

I was so excited about moving back to New York. I quickly came to learn that people, places and things can drive you right back into the insanity.

Coming home was bittersweet for me. On the one hand I did miss seeing my parents, but on the other hand, it brought back many painful memories of my childhood. My parents were still living in the same apartment in Queens, and old thoughts came rushing through my head.

My dad was now retired and spent his days staying as busy as possible. My mom was still working but also had her friends to spend time with. My dad had his daily cocktails and the crossword puzzle.

I was back in a suit and working in Manhattan, my old stomping grounds. The consulting firm I was working for had been retained to do marketing research projects for some of the biggest global communications companies. I was given the task of working with a large Japanese energy company, and my weeks were spent traveling between Washington, D.C. and New York.

I enjoyed the travel and the allure of staying in fancy hotels and having the end of the day cocktails at the hotel bar. I loved the work that I was doing. Global telecommunications companies hired my firm to help them pre-market new technologies and to find out what markets they would be best received. Working with Japanese clients is always a challenge, but I seized the opportunity. I used Japanese/English interpreters for all of my presentations, and I was well received by my client. I was spending most evenings at the Nippon Club, enjoying sushi and sake. I loved the taste of sake, and before too long, sake martinis were my new drink.

While I was off at work, my wife spent her days with my father. They would take daily walks and end the day with some cocktails. My wife would later tell me that those days were some of the best times she had. I would come home in the early evening, and we would all sit around and have some more drinks. As much as I was grateful for having a place to stay, my primary goal was to find us a place of our own as soon as possible. We were living in cramped quarters and privacy was limited.

I had been in touch with some old college buddies, and as it turned out, one of them was renting a two-bedroom apartment in a house on Long Island. He was planning on moving into the city in a few months, so he invited us to move in and split the rent. We packed up our things and moved in.

My friend was living on the north shore of Long Island, right on the Long Island Sound. It felt so good to be so close to the water. The apartment had a huge fireplace to boot. My commute to the city was longer but living on Long Island was something special.

Being back in Corporate America was definitely an eye opener. I had grown accustomed to wearing jeans to work, and now it was back to suits and ties. Along with the daily business meetings also came the daily three martini lunches. I thought that I had escaped the daily stressors of city life, but that was not the case. If anything, New York City called me back like never before. There seemed to be a bar on every block, and before I knew it, I was having daily eye openers and dreaming about the way I hoped things could be.

Reflecting back, I can see that, even though I always had good jobs, they were never good enough. I had the disease of "mores". One of anything was never enough.

At the end of the day, instead of heading back home, I would find myself at either the Top of the Sixes or the Rainbow Room drinking shots of tequila and thinking about either lost opportunities or the troubled future that seemingly lay ahead.

Why couldn't I live in the moment? I was constantly filled with anxiety about the past, things I should have done, people I had hurt; and the fear of the future.

I loved the consulting work and made some excellent contacts. I remember one payday in particular. Everyone in the office was literally running downstairs to the bank to cash their checks. I got in line and asked an associate, "why the rush?" He told me that the owner of our firm had a knack for mismanaging funds and that there were no guarantee that by the time I got to the teller, there would be enough funds available to cash my check. Now that was a real eye-opener.

I had only been back in New York for a few short months and found myself in the position of possibly having to find a new, more stable position. One of the things that I did have going for me was my list of industry contacts, and before too long, I had lined up some exciting opportunities.

I had longed to get back into the Broadcast Network arena and was eventually offered a network operations job with a British News Agency. I was ecstatic. Our offices were in the heart of Rockefeller Center, and my office window looked out on the skating rink.

The British News agency I worked for was at the leading edge of providing global news crews, and I found myself right in the middle of the "game" again. I had the opportunity to provide International satellite feeds for events like "Live Aid." I got overtaken by all of the glitz and glamor and found myself getting "lost in the shuffle." After a hard day's work, it was off to the local watering holes, always seemingly avoiding having to go home. Looking back, I had so much to be grateful for, but I was too blind to see it.

One day I was called into the General Manager's office. I was advised that the company had been purchased by Reuters and that I had one week to clean out my desk. Again, the "poor me's" set in, and drinking was the only thing I knew to help me deal with the situation. Instead of taking a deep breath and analyzing my options, I shut down and stayed stuck in feeling sorry for myself instead.

When the "fog" lifted, so to speak, I decided to start my own consulting company and to focus on using my varied global contacts to get some work. Luckily, I had built some very strong industry relationships, and before too long, I had landed some good contracts. So, here I was again, running all over the city, developing business and entertaining potential clients. I would inevitably wind up at some restaurant or bar, doing my best to line up business.

As I look back now, I can definitely see how my ego was totally in control. I was going to conquer New York.

I was fortunate enough to make some excellent deals and continued to do my best to take care of my family. I continued to burn the candle at both ends, but this beginning to take its toll on me.

The long days of hustling for business and the endless nights of partying started to wear me down. As much as I wanted to prove to everyone that I was at the top of my game, I was starting to "tumble." It became clear to me that working for yourself can be quite challenging, especially when you are not sure if you will get paid by your client's on time. I decided that that this was becoming too much of a risk and decided that I needed to go back to work for a large company that would provide the security that I needed both for myself and my family.

Chapter 5

The Telecom World

*I finally had thought that I found my niche, but unfortunately,
I still had a major ego problem and many more lessons to
learn.*

I had spent several weeks meeting with recruiters and
sending out resumes when an opportunity presented itself.
The telephone business as we know it was starting to change,
and many small independent companies were emerging and
starting to take a bite out of Mama Bell (AT&T).

A small company out of Boston, CTC (Computer Telephone
Company) was looking to get a piece of the NYC market,
and I was hired as an Account Executive for their Long
Island Branch office. We had a team of 10 sales execs who
were aggressively trying to corner the local phone company
business. At this time, CTC had worked out a reseller
agreement with NYNEX, and we were going after all the
Long Island corporations, selling them a variety of voice and
data services.

I quickly managed to land some huge contracts, and started
to make some good money and became one of the top sales

reps for our region. So you would think that I would be happy enough with this but, no, my ego once again kicked in and I decided that I wanted to make a play for a management position. Unfortunately, the timing was not right, and the opportunity did not present itself.

Even though I was not currently working in NYC, I was able to find sufficient watering holes on the Island, and the end of the day found me at my usual seat, at some barstool. Alcohol was my best friend, and I always went to her when things were not going my way.

Once again, I decided that I needed to find a better job and one that would also get me back into the city. Around this time, I received a call from a recruiter who told me that she had a position that was perfect for me with a company called MFS (Metropolitan Fiber Systems) and that they were located in the Wall Street Area. I was totally excited and asked her to set up the interview. I had an interview the following week and was offered the position.

I was all set. I was heading back to where the "big boys" played. I had been spending a good amount of time learning all I could about fiber optics, and MFS was in the process of building domestic and global networks for their clients. It wasn't too long before I was landing key accounts and pushing myself to the top of the sales leader board. More importantly, I was back in NYC and I was once again able to wine and dine clients. Sales always seemed to come easy to me, and before long, the huge monthly commission checks started rolling in.

I remember going to an ATM machine to check my balance. I thought I was dreaming when I saw my paycheck which included a $5,000 commission check. Well, you know what happened next.

After calling my wife to give her the news, I went out and celebrated. I should have gone right home, but I didn't, and I finally rolled into my home at 1:00am.

One day, my General Manager called me into his office and advised me that a management position was opening up and that the position would be to run sales offices in White Plains and Long island. I was offered the position and was ecstatic. I had finally been given the management opportunity I had been hoping for.

It took me about two weeks to put together sales teams for both locations. I had a good industry reputation and as soon as I put the word out that I was building two sales teams, the phone calls came pouring in. So, here I was, spending my time between White Plains and Long Island, with all the free time I needed.

So, again, you would think that after a hard day's work, I would look forward to going home to be with my family. No. What I did was head back into the city to spend time with my drinking buddies. The insanity started all over again. I should have been focusing more on making my sales teams more successful and being there for them, but all I could think about was drinking.

As I look back, I can see now that when times were bad, I drank, which only made things worse, and when times were good, I drank to make them better. I could never find the right balance.

I remember asking one of my dear friends, years later, why no one ever approached me about my drinking. He said me to me "we always had such a good time hanging out with you".

My sales teams excelled, and we were always being recognized for our overall performance. There were the top sales performer trips to exotic locations, and you can imagine just how much drinking went on. That's the world of sales. I continued to outperform as a sales manager and the bonus' were plentiful.

Chapter 6

Disaster strikes and the re-build

Just when I thought I had grabbed onto the golden ring, just when I felt I had finally arrived; everything came crashing down around me.

MFS was doing exceptionally well in the Global Telecom arena and before you knew it, we were scooped up by a larger company called Worldcom. Worldcom had recently purchased MCI and with the MFS purchase, had now become a Global Telecommunications giant.

Our clients were international in scope and sales really exploded. Worldcom rewarded performance with stock options and before long, I had several thousand shares of the company stock. The company continued to outperform the competition and I continued to be rewarded with more and more stock options.

I had decided at various times, after talking with my wife, to cash in some stock options so that I could help out our parents with bills, etc. As the company continued to prosper, we started receiving emails from Worldcom's financial partner, Soloman Smith Barney, strongly suggesting that employees not sell their stock options; instead, borrowing from family or friends if necessary.

I should have realized at this time that something "fishy" was going on. I had accumulated almost 50,000 stock options at the strike price of $12/share and the company stock was at the $60/per share mark. I was thirty days from being 100% vested when the roof fell in.

Overnight, Worldcom stock went to zero and the company eventually went from chapter 7 to chapter 11 and it was all over.

I remember me and my wife sitting in front of the TV set watching CNN she was drinking from a bottle of Crown Royal, and I was drinking from a bottle of Tequila. If there was ever a time for drinking and sobbing this was it. Overnight, I literally went from a six-figure salary to unemployment. Many employees were saved, but many were not. It was at this time that my drinking really took off.

My wife had a very hard time grasping what had just happened and blamed me for not properly managing my company portfolio. I was crushed and self-medication was my only salvation. I fell into a dark hole for several weeks and I just did not know what or where to go. Thankfully, my wife at the time had a great job and she now became the sole breadwinner of the family. My ego took a bashing and I just didn't see any way out.

Eventually I flashed back to the words my father had told me so many years ago, that when you get kicked to the curb, you pick yourself up and start over.

I finally was able to start thinking clearly and decided that I needed to pick myself up and get a job. The good news was that what had happened at Worldcom was not my fault and I just needed to get back in touch with the recruiters I had worked with in the past.

In no time, I landed a job as a sales manager for a company called Corporate Express. The company sold office products and they needed a sales manager for their NYC office. As I did have an excellent track record in sales management, the interview process went smoothly and was hired. The salary package I received was more than I had ever gotten, and I couldn't wait to celebrate.

My office was in the West Village and there was not a lack of restaurants and bars to choose from. I embraced my new position, but it took some time for me to gain the respect of my sales team.

They had been without a sales manager for quite some time and the sales reps all worked independently. They did not like having to come to weekly sales meetings but after a while they did come to see the benefits of being able to review all of the business we had and to brainstorm ways of increasing business. It did not take long for my sales team to become the number one team in the tri-state region and with this came the bonuses.

I became one of the top sales managers for the company and won several awards. At this time, one of our accounts was a major financial institution and one of my sales reps sold them all of their promotional items. It was a huge account, so I focused most of my attention on this account and the rep. We took many sales trips together and of course this involved wining and dining the client. I was all caught up in the success and the money.

Ever since the Worldcom nightmare, my marriage had been slipping and I just didn't know what to do or care. I had for the most part been living comfortably numb for almost thirty years. I had always been there for my son (at least I thought I had) but now it appeared as if I was lost and totally on my own.

Anyone who has been in sales knows that drinking is part of the game and if you have an expense account, all the better (or the worse). I was like a kid in the candy store. Unfortunately, my priorities got lost in the shuffle and due to some bad errors in judgement and my butting heads with my sales director, the company and I eventually parted ways. The good news was that the company General Manager had left one month earlier and had always told me to stay in touch with him, in case I ever wanted to move.

Chapter 7

The Awakening

I finally began to see that alcohol had a tight grip on me and it was slowly taking me down.

My drinking had really taken hold of me and things at home were really starting to deteriorate. My relationship with my son had all but fallen apart and my relationship with my wife at the time was pretty much over. My days were now pretty much filled with remorse, regret, and self-pity. I just couldn't get a handle on anything.

It was the morning of September 24th, 2008 and I felt like my life was over.

After getting back home from taking my son to school, I had a few drinks and wrote out my last will and testament. I was done. I emailed a copy to my childhood friend and another copy to my sister. I sat with the most horrible feeling ever, not wanting to live and not wanting to die. I had had thoughts of suicide in the past, but this time I was really scared. It seemed like an eternity, but before I knew it, my best friend called me asking me what the hell was going on. For the first time in my life, I broke down and cried and said, "I need help. I'm an alcoholic and a drug addict and I am in trouble".

My friend Peter urged me to get into my car and come to see him ASAP. I can't explain it, but I felt so relieved, saying that I was an alcoholic and addict and needed help.

I drove to White Plains to see Peter. I met him at a diner and had something to eat for the first time in what seemed months. Peter was a godsend and he helped me to find my way onto the road of recovery.

I called my doctor and made an appointment to see him later that day. I knew that I was a complete mess and that I needed help both physically and mentally. If It wasn't for my friend Peter being there for me, I would not be alive today.

When I got back home, something made me go to my son's computer and google AA. All I knew about AA was from what I had seen in the movie Clean and Sober, with Michael Keaton. I called the Nassau County Intergroup and they told me that there was a meeting later that day in my area. I felt like the weight of the world had been lifted off my shoulders. I met with my doctor and told him that I was an alcoholic and that I needed help. He told me that he pretty much knew this and had been waiting for me to admit it. Guess what? You can't hide the smell of vodka!

I went to my first AA meeting that day and I have never looked back. I was going to do whatever it took to get clean and sober and knew that I had no other choice. In addition to my drinking, my head was also a mess and I knew that I needed to find a therapist who could help me. A lady from the AA meeting referred me to her therapist and I set up an appointment.

To this day, I am indebted to this therapist who helped me to get my life back. I believe that everyone should have a therapist. Just think how much better the world would be if people had a place to go to dump their problems.

I was going to 4-5 AA meetings a day and was finally with people who understood me, loved me and without judgement. I had been judged my whole life. It felt so good. I quickly got a sponsor and started doing the work. I knew that I was in the right place.

After about one month in recovery, I decided that it was time for me to move out of my house. I knew that I needed to get sober and healthy so that I could be a good father to my son. I knew that my marriage was over. I believe that we had stayed together way too many years because of our son.

I remember going upstairs to my son's room and telling him that I needed to talk to him. I told him that I had a drinking problem and that I was getting help and needed to move out for the sake of the family.

It took six months to repair my relationship with my son. In AA, I learned all about acceptance. I sent my son a text every day telling him that I loved him and that I would always be there for him and just let it go.

Six months later, I was getting ready to walk into an AA meeting when my son texted me asking me if I wanted to get together tomorrow, which was Father's Day. Today, my son is my best friend.

After being sober for almost two months, I got a call from my old friend, the General Manager that I worked for at Corporate Express. He needed a sales manager for his company and wanted to know if I was interested. I was eager to get back to work and felt that I was strong enough in my recovery to venture back out into the world. I set up an interview for the following week.

The offices were located at 1 Penn Plaza and the location was perfect for me as I could literally walk into the building from the LIRR station. I must admit that I was a bit apprehensive, but I really needed to get back to work. The interview was more of a formality and I was offered the position. I would be managing a team of seven salespeople and would not have to leave the city for client appointments. It did not take long for the sales team to warm up to me and I was back in the saddle again.

The sales team I had inherited was one of the top teams in the region and before too long I was getting significant commission checks again. It felt good but I knew that I needed to be very cautious of my feelings and emotions.

I called my sponsor every day and one of the first things I did was to find an AA meeting close to the office. I found one that met every day at 12 and it worked out perfectly for me. Those meetings were a life saver. As time went on, I was right back in the swing of things but this time, I was able to find ways to excuse myself from company after work functions and client parties. I knew that I just could not be around alcohol.

One of the real tests came when I had to take my first sales trip to Texas. I was pretty scared about flying as I had always drunk on flights. I talked to my sponsor and felt confident that I could make the trip. The first thing I did when I got to Dallas was to find local AA meetings. So, when the sales teams went out drinking after the days meetings, I jumped into a cab and went off to a meeting.

One of the amazing things about AA is that there are meetings in every city, and I felt right at home. I made it through the trip and was grateful for being sober.

As much as I had tried to stay away from company functions, I was not able to avoid the company Christmas Party. Needless to say, the alcohol was flowing, and I had to grit my teeth to make it through the evening. Several client parties also took place around Christmas and I needed to be there. It was after the slew of parties that I realized that I had to make a very tough decision.

Chapter 8

Hard Decisions & Moving On

*I had finally come to the conclusion that that I either took
control of my life or lose it to alcohol!*

It became abundantly clear to me that being around alcohol
was no longer an option and unfortunately, sales and alcohol
seemingly go hand in hand. I spoke to my sponsor and spent
some time in deep prayer and meditation. I decided that I
could no longer be a part of corporate America and made the
decision to resign.

I met with my General Manager, who was aware that I was in
recovery. The conversation went better than expected and the
company agreed to lay me off so that I could collect
unemployment insurance. It was one of the best decisions I
ever made. I took some deep breaths and headed home.

For the next few weeks all I did was attend AA meetings. It
was where I needed to be. I had become very spiritual over
time and decided that the next step would come to me at the
right time.

My relationship with my son was better than ever and I was very grateful that we had become close again. My son gave me my first year of sobriety coin and he has since then been to all of my sober anniversaries.

One day my son came to me and asked me if I would come to his high school and talk to his friends about alcohol and drugs. My son was one of the co-captains of the football team and he told me that his friends were not taking drugs and alcohol seriously and that he felt that they needed to hear more about this. I told my son that I had no problem doing this but that he might hear some nasty things from his friends once they heard my story, as I had coached Little League Baseball in our town for many years and knew many of his classmates and their families. My son said that this didn't matter to him. We needed to try and help make a difference.

I started going into the HS and talking to the health classes about drug addiction, my son sitting right next to me. The stories that these kids told were very hard to take in. Many of them had experimented with alcohol and drugs and many of them had parents who drank to excess. The students wrote detailed letters back to their teacher and these letters were shared with me. The letters brought tears to my eyes.

I continued to have these talks with the students, and I would like to think that in some small way, I was able to help some of them deal with their issues.

One day, I was sharing some of these letters at an AA meeting that I ran. After the meeting, a lady came up to me and said, "You need to do something more". This made me think about what I should be doing next. I decided that I needed to become a drug counselor so that I could help people struggling with addiction. I did some research and found a program that provided the education necessary for the credential that I would need. As it turned out, New York State considers alcohol and drug addiction to be a disability and I received a full scholarship to attend the program.

The program was a five-month intensive program, so I was attending classes Monday through Thursday from 9-4. I felt humbled by the experience and grateful for the opportunity.

Over the next five months, I learned so much about the disease of addiction and all of the issues that go along with individuals and families struggling with drug addiction. During my studies, I also interned at one of the most reputable substance abuse outpatient programs on Long island. I eventually graduated with honors and was offered a part-time counseling position. I was working twenty hours a week, so I found another part-time position with another outpatient program so that I was now getting in forty hours a week. I was so grateful to have these positions and spent as much time as I could learning as much I could. It wasn't too long before I was facilitating my own groups. The experience I gained was invaluable.

Within three months, I was offered a full-time case manager's position with one of the facilities I was working for, Ken Peters Center for Recovery, and I had finally found what I had been looking for. I was embraced by the entire staff and I was now running my very own intensive outpatient group. As time went on, I became all the more knowledgeable of how to work with both individuals and families struggling with addiction. I was so grateful for the work I was doing.

My own recovery was going amazingly well, and I still was attending 4-5 AA meetings a week. For the next two years I found myself doing what I believed was "God's work", helping struggling addicts find peace of mind. I was never happier.

At this point I had started thinking about one day being able to do private therapy work. After doing some research, I came to the conclusion that I would need to go back to school to get my master's in social work so that I could attain the necessary license to practice.

Since graduating from Binghamton with my BA in 1976, I had remained very involved with the University as an alumni athlete. I had also been actively working with admissions and the alumni organization and thought what better school to go to than my alma mater. I found out that Binghamton had a Master's in Social Work program and set up an interview.

My son was a sophomore at Binghamton at this time, so I decided to have a conversation with him about the possibility of us being in the same school. Trevor was more than happy so things seemed to be falling into place.

I drove up to Binghamton for the interview and met with both the Dean of the school and the Director of Admissions. I could not go full time so we discussed the part time program.

It was a three-and-a-half-year program, with classes night classes twice a week. The school encouraged me to apply and also provided me with a list of local treatment centers that might be looking for case managers. I went back home and filled out the graduate application. I sent out several resumes and was quickly contacted by one of the local outpatient facilities. I was called in for an interview and was back up in Binghamton within one week.

I've since come to believe in recovery that there is a plan for all of us and that we need to have faith in that plan.

Needless to say, the interview went well. So, here we go. In two weeks' time, I was accepted to the graduate school and offered the case manager's position. So, now I had to figure out how I was going to pay for school and I also needed to find a place to live.

I decided that if my son was getting money from FAFSA so would I. I applied for the loan and was accepted. I spent two weekends up in Binghamton looking for apartments and found the ideal apartment five minutes from campus. I don't know exactly how all of this happened but I just "buckled my seatbelt" and held on tight.

My son and I had the chance to spend some amazing quality time for almost two years in Binghamton and I will always be eternally grateful for this. Fast forward three and a half years, I specialized in trauma and graduated with honors in 2016.

Chapter 9

A Second Life

One of the greatest gifts I have been given in sobriety is having the chance to live two lives in one lifetime. I had finally come out on the other side!

Before graduating, I sent out several resumes to treatment facilities back on Long Island as my plan was to get back home so that I could be close to family. My contacts came through and I was offered a case manager's job close to home. I also found an apartment that was only ten minutes from the office. Life is amazing and I owe it all to my sobriety.

On September 24th, 2019, I celebrated eleven years of living one day at a time, clean and sober.

My life is just beginning. I lost so many things when I was drinking and drugging but with sobriety I got so much more back.

More to be revealed!!!